Reshma Saujani

Published in the United States of America by Cherry Lake Publishing
Ann Arbor, Michigan
www.cherrylakepublishing.com

Reading Adviser: Marla Conn, MS, Ed, Literacy specialist, Read-Ability, Inc.
Book Designer: Jennifer Wahi
Illustrator: Jeff Bane

Photo Credits: ©DiegoMariottini/Shutterstock, 5; ©Freedomz/Shutterstock, 7; ©Fuzheado/Wikimedia/Creative Commons Attribution-Share Alike 4.0 International, 9, 22; ©wavebreakmedia/Shutterstock, 11; ©Meet the media Guru/Photo by Luca Monterosso/flickr, 13, 23; ©Stock Rocket/Shutterstock, 15; ©Women's eNews/flickr, 17; ©New America/flickr, 19; ©Alec Perkins/Wikimedia/Creative Commons Attribution 2.0 Generic, 21; Jeff Bane, cover, 1, 6, 10, 14

Library of Congress Cataloging-in-Publication Data

Names: Sarantou, Katlin, author. | Bane, Jeff, 1957- illustrator.
Title: Reshma Saujani / by Katlin Sarantou ; illustrated by Jeff Bane.
Description: Ann Arbor : Cherry Lake Publishing, [2019] | Series: My
  itty-bitty bio | Includes bibliographical references and index.
Identifiers: LCCN 2019004220| ISBN 9781534146990 (hardcover) | ISBN
  9781534148420 (pdf) | ISBN 9781534149854 (pbk.) | ISBN 9781534151284
  (hosted ebook)
Subjects: LCSH: Saujani, Reshma, | Women in computer science--Biography. |
  Women in technology--Biography. | Women lawyers--Juvenile literature. |
  Girls Who Code (Organization)--Juvenile literature.
Classification: LCC TK7885.53 .S27 2019 | DDC 340.092 [B] --dc23
LC record available at https://lccn.loc.gov/2019004220

Printed in the United States of America
Corporate Graphics

About the author: Katlin Sarantou grew up in the cornfields of Ohio. She enjoys reading and dreaming of faraway places.

About the illustrator: Jeff Bane and his two business partners own a studio along the American River in Folsom, California, home of the 1849 Gold Rush. When Jeff's not sketching or illustrating for clients, he's either swimming or kayaking in the river to relax.

I was born in Illinois in 1975.

My parents were **immigrants**.

I went to college. I studied **political science**.

I went to law school. I became a **lawyer**.

What do you want to go to school for?

I ran for **Congress** in 2010.

I was the first Indian American woman to run.

Learning is important to me.

I noticed that few girls were in computer classes.

What is something you like
to do on the computer?

In 2012, I started Girls Who Code.

The club helps girls learn more about computers.

The girls in the club learn many skills.

Some skills are **robotics** and **web design**.

What are some other skills that
would be helpful to learn?

I want girls to do well.

My goal is to teach 1 million girls to code by 2020.

I have won many awards.

One is for being a great leader.

Today, I travel. I give talks around the world.

I think girls should be leaders in **technology**.

What would you like to ask me?

2010

1970

↑
Born
1975

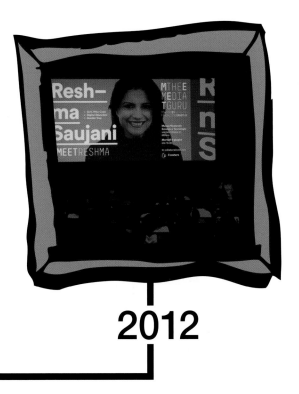

2012

2070

glossary

Congress (KAHNG-gris) the lawmaking part of the U.S. government, made up of the House of Representatives and the Senate

immigrants (IM-ih-gruhnts) people who come from a different country to live in another country

lawyer (LOI-ur) someone who practices law

political science (puh-LIT-ih-kuhl SYE-uhns) the study of government systems

robotics (roh-BAH-tiks) the design and construction of robots

technology (tek-NAH-luh-jee) a field that deals with science and engineering

web design (WEB dih-ZINE) the process of creating websites

index